THE OFFICIAL
Arsenal
ANNUAL
2004

**Compiled by
Christopher Bevan
and Joseph Cohen**

g

A Grange Publication

Published by Grange Communications Ltd., Edinburgh.
™ & © 2003 The Arsenal Football Club plc.
Licensed by Granada Commercial Ventures.
Printed in the EU.

ISBN 1-902704-50-9

£5.99

CONTENTS

FAMOUS

4

GOALS...

Down the years there have been many memorable goals scored by Arsenal players, whether it be the famous Michael Thomas winner against Liverpool in 1989, or Thierry Henry running the length of the pitch and sliding on his knees after his award-winning goal against Spurs last season at Highbury.

Here we have a look at a selection of Arsenal goals that have been well remembered, not only for being great goals, but also because the celebrations have left a lasting impression on fans.

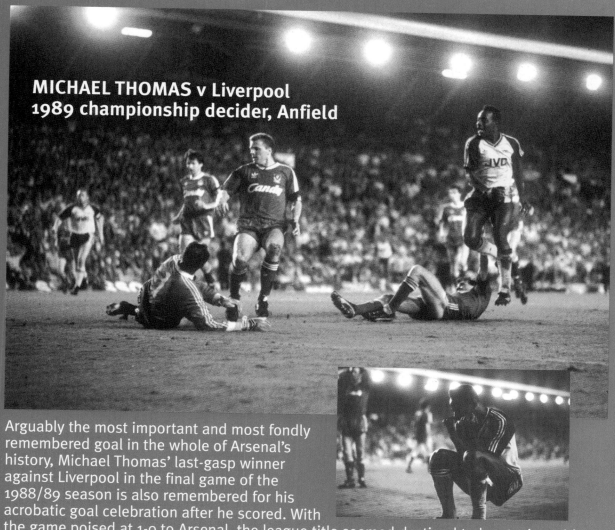

MICHAEL THOMAS v Liverpool
1989 championship decider, Anfield

Arguably the most important and most fondly remembered goal in the whole of Arsenal's history, Michael Thomas' last-gasp winner against Liverpool in the final game of the 1988/89 season is also remembered for his acrobatic goal celebration after he scored. With the game poised at 1-0 to Arsenal, the league title seemed destined to be staying with Liverpool. However in the final minute of the game up popped Thomas and coolly slipped the ball into the net to ensure that the League Championship was won by Arsenal in the most dramatic fashion imaginable.

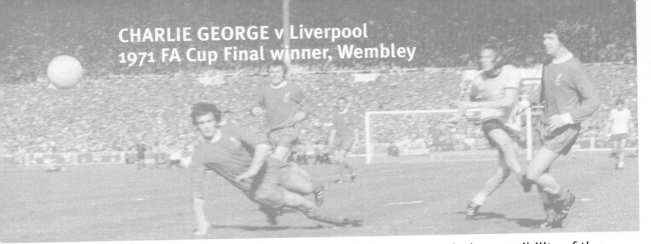

CHARLIE GEORGE v Liverpool
1971 FA Cup Final winner, Wembley

With the clock ticking away at the end of normal time, and with the possibility of the Club's first 'double' hanging in the balance, Charlie George - Arsenal's major talent of the 1971 Cup Final team crashed a thunderous drive past the Liverpool 'keeper and into the net to seal an historic victory. Instead of wheeling away in sheer delight, Charlie collapsed on to the Wembley turf and lay in the shape of a cross waiting for his team mates to come and celebrate with him. This enduring image has placed Charlie George in both Arsenal folklore and British sporting history.

ALAN SUNDERLAND v Manchester United
1979 FA Cup Final winner, Wembley

At 2-0 up with 10 minutes to play, Arsenal looked as if they were heading towards a famous FA Cup Final victory against Manchester United in the sweltering heat at Wembley. However the last ten minutes of the game saw an astonishing comeback from United as they scored two goals in as many minutes. The pressure was now on Arsenal as the momentum was with Manchester United. However Arsenal went on the counter attack in the dying minutes of the game and a Liam Brady cross was met at the far post by a sliding Alan Sunderland. He finished to win the match for Arsenal in one of the most nail-biting finishes to an FA Cup Final ever. Sunderland's celebration was full of emotion as he wheeled away with pure delight, realising that he had just scored the goal that had won the Cup for Arsenal.

TONY ADAMS v Everton 1998 sealing the Premier League, Highbury

An Arsenal victory would ensure that the Premier League would be won for the first time. Tony Adams, Arsenal's most successful Club Captain, capped off a truly memorable day when he ran on to a beautifully floated pass from his defensive counterpart, Steve Bould, and smashed an unstoppable left-footed half volley past the Everton 'keeper to seal a 4-0 victory and the Premier League trophy. Adams' celebration after scoring the goal has almost become as famous as the goal itself, as he stood in front of a delirious North Bank with his arms aloft, saluting the Highbury faithful.

IAN WRIGHT v Bolton Wanderers 1997 breaking the scoring record, Highbury

This game will go down in Arsenal history forever as it proved to be the match when Highbury legend, Ian Wright, broke the Club's all-time scoring record. 'Wrighty' netted the 179th goal of his Arsenal career to take him past the crucial milestone set by Cliff Bastin, the previous holder, more than 50 years before. His jubilation at writing himself into Arsenal's rich history was there for all to see when he displayed the tee-shirt "179 Just Done it!" after scoring the famous goal.

KANU v Chelsea
1999 remarkable 15 minute hat-trick, Stamford Bridge

With fifteen minutes left until the full-time whistle and Arsenal trailing 2-0 to London rivals Chelsea, the game looked as if it was going to end in defeat for the Gunners. That's until Arsenal's skilful Nigerian, Kanu stepped forward. Kanu scored two quick goals to put Arsenal on level terms with Chelsea and in the final minutes of the game he produced some sublime skill on the Chelsea goal line, combined with a breathtaking finish to secure an emphatic win for the Gunners at Stamford Bridge. Kanu celebrated his winning goal with a style that has become known as 'six gun salute'!

DENNIS BERGKAMP v Tottenham Hotspur
1996 settling the Derby

All North London derbies are tense affairs and this game back in the 1996/1997 season was no exception. On a wet afternoon at Highbury Dennis Bergkamp, Arsenal's mercurial Dutch striker illuminated the crowd after he scored a stunning goal in front of the North Bank. After some terrific work on the wing, Ian Wright crossed the ball into the box where it was deftly controlled by Bergkamp with his left foot. He then switched the ball

on to his right foot and crashed past the stranded Tottenham goalkeeper with supreme confidence. Dennis' reaction after scoring against Arsenal's closest rivals in such an important game was one of pure joy; he ran over toward the corner of the pitch and slid onto his knees with his fists clenched.

8

ROBERT PIRES v Aston Villa
2001/2002 lob over Schmiechel, Villa Park

During their tremendous 'double' winning season in 2001/2002, the Gunners had an awkward away trip to Villa Park to take into account. Robert Pires was having the season of his life and the goal that he scored against Aston Villa was just outstanding. Picking up a long floated through ball from Freddie Ljungberg, Pires had to beat a Villa defender before he was through on goal. He deftly lifted the ball over the head of the defender and ran around him to position himself correctly for the sublime lob he produced in over the outstretched keeper's arms. His goal celebration was understated but has become the trademark of Arsenal's terrific number 7, 'the finger wag'.

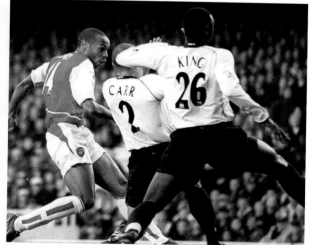

THIERRY HENRY v Tottenham Hotspur, 2002 magnificient solo effort, Highbury

Thierry Henry has become a living Arsenal legend and the goal he scored at Highbury against Tottenham in the 2002/2003 season was one of such class it has ensured that he will always be held in the hearts of Arsenal fans. Having picked the ball up in the Arsenal half of the pitch, Thierry controlled the ball expertly and then manoeuvred his way into the opposition's half at a tremendous pace, leaving midfielders in his wake. He was soon bearing down on the Tottenham defenders and it was clear that they were not going to catch him or be able to tackle him. He kinked his body to the left at the top of the penalty area and pushed the ball onto his left foot, then 'bang' he crashed the ball past the flailing goalkeeper, who could only watch as the ball arrowed into the corner of the net. Thierry's reaction to scoring such a wonderful goal amazed everyone. After he had ran the length of the pitch to score he decided to run all the way back again to end up sliding on his knees in celebration in front of the cheering fans in the West Stand.

BEHIND THE SCENES ON MATCHDAY

Before the players, officials and fans turn up at Highbury on a match day there is plenty to be done in preparation to ensure that everything from the pitch to the safety of the fans is cared for.

Here is an insider's guide to how a match day at Highbury runs from the staff who have crucial roles to play before and after the game.

Highbury Groundsman – Paul Burgess

Highbury groundsman Paul Burgess and his assistant Paul Ashcroft are responsible for ensuring that Arsenal maintain their proud tradition of having one of the finest playing surfaces in the country. We caught up with Paul as he was preparing for a Premier League game on a Saturday afternoon.

"I'll be awake at 5:30am and I make sure that I am down at the Stadium an hour later to meet with Paul. Our first task is to get straight out on to the pitch to brush the morning dew from the surface of the pitch. This will take about half an hour."

"At 7:00am we'll cut the pitch width ways. The grass is cut so that it is approximately an inch high, though when the weather is hot the grass grows quicker so we cut the grass to three quarters of an inch to allow for the growth during the day. It takes two hours to cut the pitch width ways and the exercise is then repeated, length ways, to create the criss-cross pattern. The stripes on the pitch are mainly for presentation but they also serve to help the linesmen in making offside decisions.

"At 11:00am we'll turn the sprinklers on and give the pitch a brief watering before we set out to mark the lines which, incidentally, are freshly marked for every game. At about 1pm we'll put out the temporary goals for the goalkeepers to warm up in; this helps to protect the two goalmouths as much as possible.

"An hour before kick off I'll walk the pitch to make sure that it is spotless. Sometimes the referee will chat to me before the game about the weather conditions, or perhaps the timing of when the floodlights should go on.

"At half-time Paul and I repair any damage to the pitch with seven other colleagues who work as 'divoters' helping out on a match day. At full-time we are back on the grass with our forks for about an hour and we usually leave the ground at about 11pm, although we have been known to still be here at 3am. But if the players are happy then it's all been worthwhile."

Stadium Manager – John Beattie

The safety of more than 35,000 people inside Highbury every match day is John Beattie's responsibility. We asked John how he co-ordinates the huge behind-the-scenes operation on the day of a UEFA Champions League fixture.

"I arrive at about 7:30am. By 8am My deputy, Mark Pearce, and I will be out inspecting the stadium, checking that nothing's out of place. We check for anything from something falling off a wall to not having enough paper cups at a concession unit. That takes the best part of two hours.

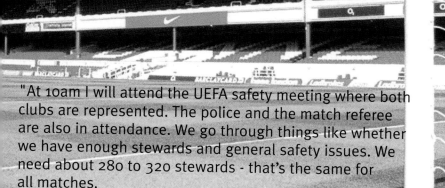

"At 10am I will attend the UEFA safety meeting where both clubs are represented. The police and the match referee are also in attendance. We go through things like whether we have enough stewards and general safety issues. We need about 280 to 320 stewards - that's the same for all matches.

"From 11am until about 4pm we're then dealing with anything that may happen on that given day. A lot of the preparation for Champions League matches has been done prior to the day of the game. For example, the press room has to be arranged to seat 150 people, the advertising boards have to change, some of the seats have to come out and other seats have to be netted.

"Come 4pm we start all the various briefings, the first of which is the internal

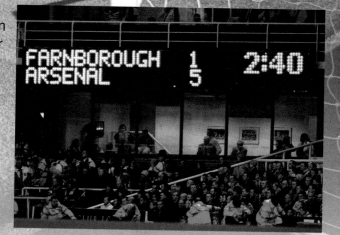

safety meeting which is attended by the Managing Director, The Club Secretary and myself. At 4:45pm I go to the police briefing. We have more police for Champions League games because they are higher risk games. At 5:30pm I will then head off to the control room which is where I run the event from.

"Once we get the okay from all the stewards we open the ground to let the fans in, usually at 6pm. Just before the kick off we're monitoring the entrances to see if there is a build up of people around certain entrances, and whether we have to delay the kick-off time. That is a decision we don't want to take for obvious reasons but if we have to take it then it is decided between the police and I.

"During the game we watch the crowd and the stewards to ensure that all is running smoothly and safely. We stay in the control room until roughly 10:30pm when we have a final inspection of the stadium, a final check that everything is okay. At about 11:15pm we have the UEFA debrief with all the UEFA officials and we normally get away from Highbury by 12:30am."

Official Club Photographer – Stuart MacFarlane

Arsenal's official Club Photographer is responsible for the vast majority of photographs you see in the Arsenal Magazine, match day programme and this annual. We caught up with Stuart recently and asked him about a typical match day. "Before kick off pictures need to be taken with mascots and matchball sponsors and there are always presentations around the ground that may need my services.

"The last thing I do, moments before kick off, is take a picture of the captains, mascots and officials in the centre circle then I have to rush to the end of ground which Arsenal are attacking and take my position behind the goal.

"At half-time I shoot up to my office and develop some of the film and after the game I'm straight up there as well. I have my own processing machine in my office, which is located in the East Stand. I put the negatives on a light box and see what the images I've taken from the day's game are like!

"The roof cameras give a great view of Highbury and those pictures become more and more significant historically as our move to the new stadium gets ever closer.

"I get a small selection of pictures developed and sent to our website, www.arsenal.com within half-an-hour, though sometimes other things might pop up post-match, like programme competition winners for example.

"If there are plenty of images that need developing and scanning then I can be working at the ground for a number of hours after the final whistle has blown."

Ground Staff – Paddy Galligan

Patrick 'Paddy' Galligan has been a member of the ground staff at Highbury since 1978. He talked us through his schedule on a busy match day.

"I arrive at 7am and my first job is to check all the dressing rooms, make sure they are all clean and ready for when the players arrive.

"I'll also go to the South Stand, check all the executive

boxes and make sure they are unlocked and ready. It's then up on to the roofs to check all the 16 flags which I have put into position the day before the game.

"Outside the ground I need to change all the match day signs, making sure they correctly set out the Club's forthcoming fixtures.

"The players usually turn up at Highbury in the early morning, sometimes even the night before if there is an afternoon kick off on a weekend fixture. They all drive to the ground in their cars and then get on a coach to take them to a hotel. Once they have left, I head back to the changing rooms to give them a quick tidy up. After that there's time for a quick sandwich and a cup of tea before looking at anything else that might need doing before kick off - like fixing seats for example.

"The players will return to the stadium about an hour before kick off. Up until then I spend my time ensuring that everything is spotlessly clean for them. I'll even offer them a cup of tea if they fancy one.

"When the players get into the changing room they put on the stereo and play their music - usually dance, not the sort of music I recognise or like very much! The important thing is that it helps them relax and prepare for the game ahead.

"Another responsibility of mine is to check the turnstile count after kick-off and at half-time. During half-time the players will have a cup of tea or an energy drink, and there are baskets of fruit as well if they require it. After they are back on the pitch for the beginning of the second half I'll be in the changing rooms giving them a final tidy and making sure they are clean for the players' return at full-time.

"After the match has finished and the players have changed they usually head home and that's when I crack on with a final tidy up. It's usually muddy after the game especially in the winter months, but nothing like it was in days gone by when the pitch wasn't the quality it is now."

2002/2003
SEASON REVIEW

A victory at Cardiff and more silverware started and finished the 2002/2003 season for the Gunners. In between there were 119 stunning Arsenal goals, many moments of fantastic football and records kept on tumbling.

MUNITY SHIELD
HIP WITH McDONALD'S
NERS 2002

August

The 2002/2003 season started as the previous season had finished, with the Gunners adding more silverware to their trophy cabinet. Brazilian World Cup winner Gilberto capped his competitive debut with the winner in a 1-0 victory over Liverpool in The FA Community Shield at the Millennium Stadium. It was a deserved victory. Liverpool goalkeeper, Jerzy Dudek, produced many great saves before Gilberto's sweet drive 20 minutes from time. The Premiership campaign kicked off with a sound 2-0 home win over Birmingham City. After an early Henry free-kick crept under Nico Vaesen, a great run and finish from Sylvain Wiltord sealed the Club's 14th straight win in the Premiership, a new all-time record for top flight football in England. A hard-fought point at West Ham, sealed by a David Seaman penalty save and a stunning blast from Henry was followed by a 5-2 home victory against West Bromwich Albion to put Arsenal firmly on top of the league.

September

Arsenal salvaged a point at Chelsea from a Kolo Toure header to earn a 1-1 draw, then put Manchester City to the sword with a tenth straight win at Highbury, a new club record. A 3-0 win at Charlton was followed by a last minute winner by Kanu at home to Bolton Wanderers. At Leeds United, an early Kanu strike set up a breathtaking 4-1 victory. One newspaper said afterwards of Arsenal: 'They're unbelievable. They are unforgettable, unassailable, unstoppable... How do you describe this unrelenting record-breaking Arsenal side?' It meant Arsenal had scored in their 47th consecutive league game, beating Chesterfield's record which had stood

since 1930. It also made it 23 Premiership away games unbeaten, beating the all-time top flight record of 22 matches held by Nottingham Forest since 1978.

In the Champions League both Borussia Dortmund (home) and PSV Endhoven (away) were beaten, 2-0 and 4-0 respectively, as Arsenal started their European campaign in exciting style.

October

Auxerre away was the only victory in a tough month. A Gilberto strike just after half-time secured the points in the compact Stade Abbe Deschamps stadium. 16-year-old whiz kid Wayne Rooney's unstoppable last minute winner for Everton at Goodison Park brought Arsenal's record-breaking run to a halt. Home defeats to Auxerre and Blackburn Rovers and away at Borussia Dortmund saw Arsenal fans looking forward to November!

November

Winning ways were resumed in Arsenal's 3,500th top-flight game. A Steve Marlet own goal secured a narrow 1-0 victory at Loftus Road against Fulham. A happy Arsène Wenger said: "We were under big pressure today, it was a must win game. We had to get three points and the character and resilience of our performance showed that the hunger is still there." A run of four home matches in 11 days started with a narrow defeat in the Worthington Cup to Sunderland. Shortly after, Newcastle were the next visitors to Highbury. Wiltord tapped in a cross from the impressive Luzhny, to seal a fine performance. A scoreless draw against PSV at Highbury sealed Arsenal's position at the top of Group A in the UEFA Champions League. Tottenham came to Highbury four days later for the 131st League derby and were met by a determined Arsenal side. In the end, Arsène Wenger's men won 3-0, but it so easily could have been more. Sylvain Wiltord had a goal ruled out for offside and Henry had an effort cleared off the line. It was one-way traffic and the deadlock was broken by an amazing solo goal by Henry. Beating several men on a 60 yard dash, Henry fired past Kasey Keller. Fantastic flowing football saw Freddie Ljungberg and Wiltord put the icing on the cake.

Despite a magnificent Dennis Bergkamp goal opening the scoring at Southampton, a James Beattie brace led to a narrow defeat for the Gunners. Arsenal's Champions League campaign recommenced in Roma with the opening fixture in stage-two. A classic Thierry Henry hat-trick mixed with some resolute defending got Stage Two of Arsenal's Champion League campaign off to a flyer. Henry's fourth and fifth goals of the week saw off a determined Aston Villa at Highbury in a 3-1 victory.

December

Three huge games in early December started with an under-par Arsenal rueing missed early chances at Old Trafford. Paul Scholes' neat finish followed a Juan Veron opener to complete a disappointing day for the Gunners. A few days later Arsenal found Valencia's stand-in goalkeeper an unbeatable force at Highbury, and the Spanish Champions held out with 10 men for the last 20 minutes. The second north London derby in a month saw the spoils shared. Arsenal weathered a first-half storm before securing a point with a cool Robert Pires penalty. A comfortable win at home to Middlesborough, a hard-fought win at West Bromwich Albion, sealed by a close range Francis Jeffers effort and a 1-1 draw with Liverpool put the Gunners five points clear at the top of the Premiership going into 2003.

January

Arsenal survived a frantic last five minutes to beat Chelsea 3-2. Gio van Bronckhorst's first goal of the season was enough to secure three points and keep the advantage at the top of the league. The FA Cup campaign began with a 2-0 home victory over Oxford United. The day will be remembered for Dennis Bergkamp notching up his 100th Gunners goal. He lifted the ball over the keeper in front of

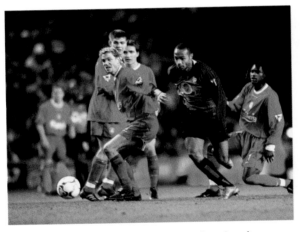

an ecstatic North Bank crowd. Next up was a convincing 4-0 away at Birmingham City. The Gunners were unaffected by a 25 minute delay due to floodlight failure. Henry was electric, bagging a brace to reach his landmark 100th goal for Arsenal too. He then made a start on his next 100 by bagging his third hat-trick in Arsenal colours against West Ham. It was the perfect hat-trick, one with the right foot; a header from Bergkamp's inch-perfect cross; and a left-footed strike after a lightening fast break. After non-league Farnborough Town were beaten 5-1 at Highbury, the Gunners travelled to Anfield. They returned with just one point

despite a fantastic performance of fast flowing football. Pires blasted the opener after great play from Bergkamp and Henry. Riise lashed an equaliser from 15 yards before Bergkamp regained the lead with a 20 yard effort. Once again the Gunners had chances to make the game safe but Liverpool made them pay when Heskey rose free at the far post to head a right wing cross beyond Seaman.

February

Two Pires efforts gave Arsenal all three points against Fulham, with the Highbury faithful waiting until the dying minutes for the winner. There were shared spoils at Newcastle, despite the hosts playing with 10 men for the last half hour. The champions took the lead when Wiltord brilliantly fed Henry in the box. His first touch took the ball past Given and his second tucked the ball into the empty net. The Magpies levelled with a rasping 25-yard Laurent Robert strike. A trip to Old Trafford saw Arsenal book their place in the last eight of the FA Cup. The first clear cut chance of the match fell to United when Giggs skipped past Seaman, then side-stepped Campbell to leave himself with an open goal, but the winger failed to keep his shot down and the ball sailed over the bar. A few minutes later the Gunners took the lead as Edu's deflected free-kick left Fabien Barthez well-beaten. Early in the second-half the Gunners doubled the lead. A twelve-pass move ended with Edu slipping the ball through to Wiltord who beat Wes Brown before putting the ball past a flat footed Barthez to put the FA Cup holders through 2-0.

On a bitterly cold London night, Arsenal started brightly against a young Ajax side with a fifth minute Wiltord strike. But a rapid response from the Dutch visitors saw them leave with one point and put three teams on five points in Arsenal's group in the phase. The 0-0 return leg against Ajax in Amsterdam was sandwiched by another trip to Manchester, this time against City, when a four-goal blitz in the opening twenty minutes set up a 5-1 success, the Gunners biggest away win for nearly four years.

MARCH

A comfortable win at home to Charlton was followed by an epic FA Cup Quarter-Final with Chelsea at Highbury. The visitors took the lead when John Terry was left all alone in the Arsenal penalty area and he placed his header beyond Seaman. Carlo Cudicini saved Henry's penalty before Jeffers bundled in the leveller. Henry put the Gunners in pole position with another masterpiece. The in-form striker controlling a pass from Vieira, spinning past Cudicini and slotting the ball home for another

goal of the season contender. But it wasn't the match winner as Frank Lampard prodded home an equaliser after a goalmouth scramble in the final ten minutes.

The Gunners were again made to pay for a succession of missed chances in the Champions League, as Roma, 1-0 down and with 10 men scrambled a point. The Gunners' 20-game unbeaten run came to an end with Blackburn Rovers becoming the first side to do the Double over the Champions since the 1999/2000 season.

Arsenal's Champions League dream ended in Spain against Valencia when they lost 1-2 and therefore failed to qualify for the Quarter-Final stage. A fifth straight Premiership home victory put the Gunners back on track against Everton. Another classic match against Chelsea followed in the FA Cup Quarter-Final replay just 48 hours later. A fantastic counter-attacking display saw Arsenal win 3-1 and march to their 23rd FA Cup Semi-Final, in the process knocking Chelsea out of the FA Cup for the third year in a row.

APRIL

A hard-fought draw at Aston Villa was quickly followed by a narrow victory against First Division Sheffield United to secure a record breaking 16th FA Cup Final place.

On Wednesday 16th April, the attention of the football world turned to Highbury for the clash between the Gunners and Manchester United. United drew first blood in the most eagerly awaited fixture of the season, going ahead in the 24th minute. Ruud Van Nistlerooy raced away from Campbell on the left and deftly beat Stuart Taylor in a one-on-one. Early in the second-half, Arsenal drew level when Ashley Cole burst into the box and his shot was deflected past Barthez by Henry. Arsenal now had the momentum and went ahead when Henry coolly slotted the ball home from Gilberto's pass. Just moments later with the home fans still on their feet, Giggs headed to make it 2-2. With a few minutes to go Arsenal nearly won it but Henry's fierce low drive was saved by Barthez. So the two sides settled for a point

apiece leaving Arsenal three points behind Manchester United but with a game in hand. A few days later, Arsenal overcame a tricky fixture at a blustery Riverside Stadium with a determined victory over Middlesborough. The points were sealed with Henry's 23rd league goal of the season, a fantastic curling free-kick. A week later, the Gunners faced another difficult away game at the Reebok Stadium against Bolton Wanderers. After a quiet first-half a neat Wiltord effort put the Champions ahead before Pires securing the points by making it 2-0. However with three forced changes: Pascal Cygan, Freddie Ljungberg and Lauren all injured in the space of fifteen minutes, Arsenal were disrupted. Youri Djorkaeff halved the deficit, and then an unfortunate Martin Keown own-goal made it 2-2, taking the destiny of the league title out of Arsenal's hands.

MAY

Only a victory at home to Leeds United would have kept the title race alive. Despite having 22 shots at goal and hitting the woodwork on several occasions, the bid to retain the championship ended with a late Mark Viduka effort and a 2-3 Leeds win.

Hat-tricks from Jermaine Pennant, Pires and Ljungberg swept away some of the championship frustrations and boosted confidence before the FA Cup Final as the Gunners fired, beating Southampton 6-1 at Highbury, followed by a convincing 4-0 victory over relegated Sunderland at the Stadium of Light. The final total of 78 points was the joint second highest of Arsène Wenger's reign and the 85 goals scored were Arsenal's highest since the 1963/64 season.

Arsenal's fourth FA Cup Final in six years saw them up against Southampton who hadn't made it that far since 1976. The match almost started in historic fashion as Henry raced clear only to be denied by Antti Niemi with little over 20 seconds on the clock. In the end it took until the 38th minute for the Gunners to break the deadlock. Fantastic skill by Henry released Bergkamp. The Dutchman switched the ball inside to Ljungberg and from there it rebounded into the path of Pires who made no mistake in firing past Niemi. Henry, Bergkamp and Pires were then all thwarted by the acrobatic brilliance of the blonde stopper. Southampton substitute 'keeper Paul Jones then took over when Niemi went off injured and he continued to defy Arsenal for the final 30 minutes. In the end, it took a world-class save from David Seaman in his last Arsenal appearance and an Ashley Cole goal-line clearance to prevent the game going into extra-time. It was a deserved victory and a deserved end to a fine season.

FA Cup Winners

Barclaycard Premiership runners-up

**Automatic qualification for the UEFA Champions League
for the sixth consecutive season**

Thierry Henry
Football Writers' Association Player of the Season 2002/2003
PFA Players' Player of the Season 2002/2003

**Arsenal Players in PFA Premier League
Team of the Season 2002/2003:**
Ashley Cole
Sol Campbell
Robert Pires
Patrick Vieira
Thierry Henry

Barclaycard Player of the Month
August - Sylvain Wiltord
September – Thierry Henry
February – Robert Pires

ITV's 'The Premiership' Goal of the Month
August Thierry Henry (vs. West Ham United)
November Thierry Henry (vs. Tottenham Hotspur)
February Thierry Henry (vs. Manchester City)

**ITV's 'The Premiership' Goal of the Season
2002/2003**
Thierry Henry (vs Tottenham Hotspur – November 2002)

ACHIEVEMENTS

**Celebration of ten years of the FA Premier League –
All time best XI's:**
David Seaman (domestic team)
Tony Adams (domestic team)
Freddie Ljungberg (overseas team)
Robert Pires (overseas team)
Patrick Vieira (overseas team)
Thierry Henry (overseas team)

Consecutive wins in the top flight of British football
14 – Set against Birmingham City on August 18, 2002

Premiership record for unbeaten matches
30 – Set against Sunderland on October 6, 2002.

All time league away record for unbeaten away matches
23 – Set against Leeds United on September 28, 2002

All time league record for scoring in consecutive matches
55 – Set against Aston Villa on November 30, 2002

Fastest Ever Champions League goal
Gilberto's goal after just 20.07 seconds against PSV Eindhoven on
September 25, 2002

Club record for consecutive home victories in the Premiership
10 set against Manchester City on September 10, 2002.

IT'S UP FOR GRABS!

it's like a tale straight out of Hollywood, every time you hear it, it just gets better...

It seemed that the hard part had been done. All Arsenal needed to do was win their last two home games – against Derby County and Wimbledon – and the League Championship would have been all but over. But football as a famous old television pundit said 'Is a funny old game'. Arsenal with a great home record until then got just one point from those two games. Now it had changed. There was one game left which was between the top two teams in the League - Liverpool and Arsenal at Anfield. All Liverpool had to do was avoid defeat by two goals and they would be Champions. They had conquered almost all before them for almost a decade. For only the third time in history, the top two were to meet on the last day with the League Championship unsettled.

Friday 26 May 1989. The kick off was delayed by traffic jams, an audience around the world waited eagerly by their television sets. When the game started Arsenal, who had not won the League Championship for 18 years, battled bravely against their superstar opponents. Rush, Aldridge, Barnes and Beardsley were just a few of Liverpool's household names. Arsenal attacked, the tackling was ferocious. One reporter said 'rarely can English football have been played with such intensity'. Chances were few and far between. A beautiful Michael Thomas cross was headed by Steve Bould, the ball arrowed towards goal but Steve Nicol, the experienced Liverpool defender, appeared from nowhere to head off the line. Then on 52 minutes, Arsenal won a free kick on the edge of the Liverpool area. Nigel Winterburn crossed, and Alan Smith suddenly appeared to flick the ball home. The linesman had flagged. 10 million people held their breath. The referee and his assistant held court. 1-0 to Arsenal. But as time ticked on and the Kop whistled, it looked as if Liverpool were on course for the 'double' and a place in the history books. One last time, Smith controlled a pass and played the ball on to Thomas. The clock stood at 91 minutes and 26 seconds. A Nicol tackle bounced against Thomas. He was clear. Grobbelaar spread himself. Time stood still. The Commentator famously screamed 'It's up for grabs now'. The Arsenal midfielder flicked the ball over the keeper. As Thomas somersaulted in shock and euphoria, the title was back in north London. It was the most dramatic end to a season ever!

DID YOU KNOW?
The actual boots Michael Thomas wore at Anfield on that famous night are now in the Arsenal Museum at Highbury! (Call 020 7704 4504 to book a stadium tour – Adults £8 / under 16s £4)

HERBERT CHAPMAN

Some say the legendary Arsenal manager, Herbert Chapman was one of the greatest managers of all-time. However, what made him all the more amazing was his apparent ability to predict the future!

▶ When he arrived at Highbury in May 1925, Chapman said it would take five years to build a winning team. Five years to the week he won The FA Cup.

▶ He introduced the idea of numbers on shirts. The Football Association listened to his proposal and numbers on shirts were first used in the 1933 FA Cup Final between Everton and Manchester City, where one team wore 1 to 11 and the other 12 to 22!

▶ He suggested the idea of the 10-yard penalty semi-circle ten years before it was finally adopted.

▶ He proposed two referees, one in each half. This concept has recently been tested by FIFA in official Youth Internationals.

▶ The England team for International matches used to be picked by committee members. Chapman argued that England would be more successful with just one manager picking the team. Once Walter Winterburn was appointed the first England manager in the 1950s, it took only a decade for England to win the World Cup in 1966.

Did you know?

In 1932 Mr Chapman's persuasive abilities convinced the local authorities to change the name of the local tube station from Gillespie Road to Arsenal. He felt this name change would create more awareness of the Club. Visitors to Arsenal station today, can still see the old Gillespie Road markings on the platforms.

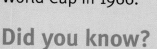

Arsenal
CENTURIONS

It may be very difficult to compare football legends from different decades and different centuries but the number of goals a striker scores can lead to membership of an exclusive club. Only 16 members to date are in the Arsenal 100 Club. In 2003, two Arsenal players, Dennis Bergkamp and Thierry Henry put their names in the record books forever after they both scored 100 goals for Arsenal.

Did You Know?
Both Dennis Bergkamp and Thierry Henry scored their first Arsenal goals against Southampton.

On joining the 100 Club
DB: I think it's quite something, especially nowadays because you need to stay at a club for a few years to achieve it. It is something that you can say I'm quite happy about. It was a very special moment to score my 100th goal and it didn't matter to me who it came against. It is 100 goals in all competitions, a historic moment for me and the Club and a proud occasion in my career. The enjoyment of scoring never leaves you and I still get the same excitement from finding the net.

TH: It's a very special achievement. Scoring 100 goals means a lot to me. I owe a lot to Arsène Wenger for this, but also to my team-mates because they have made it all possible. I didn't think I was going to reach the hundred, it came really quickly. When I was at Juventus I didn't think my career was going that way. But Arsenal gave me a hand and this is the only way I have to thank them. You have to give credit to the players I play with. To reach that mark is impossible without good players around you. To score 100 for one team is great, it's really something. It's a great feeling. Look at the people who have done it. Look at the dates of the people who scored 100 here. Apart from Wrighty and Alan Smith, it goes back to the 1920s. To do it in the modern game, well what can I say, it's an amazing feeling!

On each others goals

Dennis on Thierry's goals:
He makes it look so easy with the inside of his foot. He has amazing pace but still keeps control and can keep relaxed at the moment he shoots. At that moment you have to have perfect balance and that's something I really admire. It's not easy when you are at full speed to keep control, and he has scored many goals like that, so you could pick any of those. Thierry's one against Spurs, for example, shows how he's in control. When lesser players run with the ball they lose it or are not always thinking about the next step. Thierry's always in control, always balanced, you can't defend against it.

Thierry on Dennis's goals:
There are a lot of Dennis's goals that I would have liked to have scored! One thing I must also say about him is that he is quite quick. Also his touch on the ball is amazing. I've never seen a player like it. I loved his goal against Newcastle in 2002. There are not many players who could have scored that goal. Not only to score it but to think about doing it. That is the difference between a great player and a normal player. Dennis knew exactly what he wanted to do.

Trademark goals

DB: What I can do is control the ball, maybe take a defender on, and then try to curl it beyond the 'keeper.

TH: A lot of the goals that I score are with the inside of my foot. I always try to put the ball really far wide of the goalkeeper. They know where I am going to put the ball, and I know, everyone knows but if you do it really well it goes in. The net is quite big and if you place it well there is no way the goalkeeper will get the ball. When I miss an opportunity like that I don't say the goalkeeper did well, I say that I did wrong because I didn't do enough. Goalkeepers know there is nothing they can do. If they move too early to try to save it then I just shoot inside the other post.

Favourite celebration

DB: I remember the one after I scored against Tottenham at home. We won 3-1 in 1996 and the game had everything. There was a bit of rain and I slid on my knees after scoring. It is perhaps not typical of how I celebrate but it was the emotion I had that day and with all the importance of the game, it was a special was to celebrate.

TH: Mine has to be against Spurs too when we won 3-0 in 2002. I ran all the way down the pitch towards the Clock End and slid on my knees.

We get on well off the pitch too

DB: We both like NBA basketball. When we talk about football we can talk on a certain level because we have the same ideas and understanding. We notice little things in games that other people may not notice.

TH: We both see the game the same way. Sometimes during a match we don't have to speak to each other, we can just give each other a knowing look!

DENNIS' FAVOURITE FIVE

Arsenal v Southampton 23/9/95

My first goal for Arsenal – and boy was it a thrill when it went in! There was a lot of pressure on me with the papers running 'Bergkamp Watch' features... asking me how many hours it would take me to score. I remember running away from the goal with all the pressure coming off my shoulders.

Arsenal v Bolton 5/5/96

That first season wasn't quite as successful as I'd have hoped. We went into the final weekend against Bolton needing a win to qualify for Europe. With just a few minutes left, I scored the winner. It wasn't a bad strike at all, but again I remember this goal for what it achieved for us rather than the quality of the strike. I wanted to deliver something to the fans and this I had.

Sunderland v Arsenal 15/1/97

One of the best goals I've ever scored. An FA Cup replay on one of those cold windy nights up north that foreign players can't cope with! I trust this effort shows what a load of rubbish such opinions are. I got the ball on the edge of their area, beat a couple of defenders and curled it perfectly into the top corner.

Leicester v Arsenal 27/8/97

My most-played Arsenal goal – just a pity it couldn't have been the winner! All the same, it crowned a near perfect hat-trick for me. I received the ball, flicked it over Matt Elliott, turned and broke free. Then I had to finish ... and I did so in style.

Newcastle v Arsenal 2/3/02

And to think some people had the cheek to ask whether I meant it! As I often do with great goals I had almost a painting in my mind of how it should go. It went exactly as I hoped. I wrong-footed the defender, danced around him ... and finished.

Did You Know?

It took Dennis Bergkamp 296 games to reach his century and Thierry Henry 181 games.

Did you know?

Bergkamp became the 15th Gunner to reach the landmark 100 goals on January 4th 2003 when he opened the scoring against Oxford United in the third round of the FA Cup at Highbury. Henry scored his milestone goal just eight days later in the 4-0 win at Birmingham City.

Bergkamp and Henry's first 100 hundred goals for the Club include 'Goal of the Season' winners in four out of the last six seasons. These were:

November 16 2002. Arsenal 3 Tottenham 0 Henry picked up the ball midway in his own half and ran at the Spurs defence. He accelerated away from the chasing Matthew Etherington before wrong footing both Ledley King and Stephen Carr. Last season's Golden Boot winner then capped the 65 yard sprint with a sweet left foot finish, low into the corner beyond the diving Kasey Keller. Henry immediately ran the length of the pitch again in celebration.

March 2 2002. Newcastle 0 Arsenal 2 Robert Pires played the ball forward to Bergkamp, who was tightly marked by Nikos Dabizas. The Dutchman flicked the ball one side of Dabizas and turned him on the other before firing past Shay Given low into the corner of the goal.

October 1 2000. Arsenal 1 Man Utd 0 Henry's amazing winner in front of the Clock End. There seemed to be little on when he received the ball just outside the penalty area with his back to goal. But he teed the ball up, turned and sent a right footed volley over a stunned Fabien Barthez into the top corner of the goal.

August 27 1997. Premiership Leicester 3 Arsenal 3: Bergkamp scored all three goals for Arsenal at Filbert Street, but his winner was a real classic. When the ball came to him inside the area, the Dutch master cushioned the pass on the outside of his right foot, and the flicked it past Matt Elliot with his left. He then took one more touch to control the ball before slamming it past Kasey Keller.

PFA Players' Player of the Season
1998 Dennis Bergkamp
2003 Thierry Henry

Football Writers' Association Player of the Season
1998 Dennis Bergkamp
2003 Thierry Henry

Others in the '100 Club'
Ian Wright. This sensational showman bagged 185 goals in 278 games and celebrated most of them in his own unique style. His awesome pace and finishing skills make him the all-time Arsenal top scorer.

Big **John Radford** had a great habit of notching up late goals in important games. Fit, fast, big and strong he even played in goal in an FA Cup semi-final for the Gunners!

It was **Alan Smith's** rocket-shot that won the Cup Winners Cup against star-studded Parma in 1994. His all-round team play was just as important as his goal scoring throughout the hugely successful late 80s and early 90s.

Did you know?

Alan Smith now hopes to teach the next generation of Centurions by coaching at the Arsenal Soccer Schools held during school holidays (call 020 7704 4142 for details)

Some said that when Frank Stapleton left Highbury for Manchester United he was as good as any centre-forward in Europe. His thunderbolt feet and amazing ability at heading the ball shot him into the all-time Arsenal scorers list.

Also available on video and DVD from Granada Video/VCI: Arsenal Centurions - 100 Goals Each from Bergkamp & Henry; and The Official History of Arsenal

WHO AM I?

1   I made my debut in November 2001 in the League Cup game at Highbury against Grimsby Town.
I was born in 1983 in Rambouillet in France.
Although injury hampered my season in 2002/2003 I hope to make my mark in 2003/2004.
Like Nicolas Anelka and a current Arsenal player I graduated from the renowned Clairefontaine Academy in France.

2   My squad number is 23.
I have appeared in the 1998 and 2002 World Cups.
I have won three trophies in my time at Arsenal.
My year of birth is 1974.

3 I turned professional in November 1998
I played for Crystal Palace on loan.
My England caps are now in double figures.
I used to go to Arsenal Soccer Schools before I was 10 years old.

4 I was born in Oxford.
I am in my second spell at Highbury.
I made my debut for Arsenal against West Bromwich Albion in 1985.
My other clubs include a Merseyside and a Midlands team.

5 I made my Arsenal debut at Sunderland's Stadium of Light.
I have played in Spain.
My country won the African Nations Cup in 2002.
I wear an old coin in my sock during Arsenal games.

6 My birthday is 15 January 1983.
I can play centre-half, midfield or fullback.
My home country is in Scandinavia.
I made my debut as a substitute against Grimsby Town in the
League Cup in November 2001.

7 I have played in three FA Cup Finals – scoring in two of them.
Before I signed for Arsenal I used to play for my home-town club.
I have scored more than 40 goals for the Gunners.
I made my Arsenal debut against Manchester United in 1998
I played for my country in the last World Cup.

8 I made my Arsenal debut as an 18 year old in a League game against
Sheffield Wednesday.
I have played in France and in Italy.
I have a World Cup winner's medal.
I have made over 300 Arsenal appearances.

9 I made my Arsenal debut in August 1999.
I have also played in France and in Italy.
I have a World Cup winner's medal.
I was once named PFA Player of the Year and Football Writer's Player
of the Year in the same season.

ANSWERS
1 JEREMIE ALLIADIERE, 2 SOL CAMPBELL, 3 ASHLEY COLE, 4 MARTIN KEOWN, 5 LAUREN, 6 SEBASTIAN SVARD,
7 FREDDIE LJUNGBERG, 8 PATRICK VIEIRA, 9 THIERRY HENRY

JUNIOR GUNNERS

The Junior Gunners started back in 1983 - 20 years ago this summer! Back then there were just 300 members. We reached an all time high of 20,000 members not so long ago. We always try to get you involved in as much as possible with trips to other clubs in the Premiership and abroad, competitions, parades, fun days etc. You won't know how good these have been unless you have taken part.

Perhaps the pinnacle in the career of any Junior Gunner is being selected as mascot for the first team. There have been hundreds of lucky JGs who have led the team out over the last 20 years, but the very first was Daniel Quy - who now works for Arsenal!

"I still remember that special day so clearly. Mascots are drawn at random from all current Junior Gunners and as the membership had only just been" launched I was chosen from around 300 members!! The game I was selected for was the first home game of the new season against Luton (it was also the day Charlie Nicholas made his home debut) - right back in 1983.
"When you see mascots they usually run out with the team but I was carried out by the Manager at the time who was Terry Neill. The team went on to win 2-1 that day and I think that as a mascot if your team wins then you feel that you have brought the team a bit more luck. After the game we went to the player's lounge where I got a ball signed by both teams.
"Now I work here and by knowing how mascots work nothing has changed one bit from the time I was mascot. We still draw them at random, give them four tickets for family and friends, let them keep the kit and give them players lounge passes for after the game."

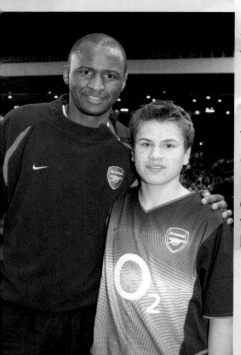

Junior Gunner Tom Clarke was one recent winner as an Arsenal away mascot

"I would just like to say thank you very, very, very much for such a brilliant day out at Liverpool on Wednesday, January 29 and enabling one of my dreams to come true.

"Two weeks earlier when I received the letter I couldn't believe it. I had forgotten all about it after I put my name down on the waiting list five years ago. I was so excited that I made my mum take me on my paper round because I was in a state of shock!

"The next school day when I told my mates, some wouldn't believe me, so I brought in the papers proving it and some of them were very excited for me. One of my friends even bought Sky Sports for the month just to watch me!

"The next two weeks were perhaps some of the longest I have experienced and the day couldn't come quickly enough. The nerves didn't really hit me until the day before my big event when I was counting down the hours.

"The next day my dad, my sister, my French lodger and I left our house in Thornbury, Bristol at about 10 am. We got to Anfield about an hour and 45 minutes before the game as I had to report to the main reception 30 minutes later. We brought a few programmes and found myself mentioned along with the Liverpool mascot. I was then invited into the Arsenal dressing room and taken round to meet the players who all signed my shirt. I even got Arsène Wenger's signature who was in the middle of planning an interview with a Sky Sports presenter. It was really interesting to catch a glimpse of what goes on behind the scenes and the atmosphere of the dressing room.

"After a while I was invited to the top of the tunnel where my dad and the Liverpool photographer took some photos of me. The Arsenal photographer then invited me onto the pitch to watch the Arsenal team warm up and to take some pictures with a few of my favourite players. I then followed the players back into the tunnel where I had a short conversation with Stuart Taylor. The players then went back to the changing room to have the final team talk and I was left standing in the tunnel with the other mascot, our families and the camera crew. I was trembling at the thought of leading my heroes out into such a tremendous stadium.

"Eventually the two teams emerged. 'This is it,' I thought, 'my two minutes of fame!' I didn't realise the camera was then filming me; I was too busy star spotting! The referee then led the way down the steps onto the hallowed turf where another cameraman was filming me coming out. I then ran to the centre spot where I and the team clapped the crowd. Next I ran off to shoot past David Seaman. This lasted for what seemed like an age until I ran back to the centre spot to have a photo with the referee, his assistants and the two captains. My two minutes were up and I ran off the pitch to watch a thoroughly entertaining 2-2 draw.

"The next afternoon I must have been the most popular kid at school. Everyone wanted to touch my shoulders where Patrick Vieira had touched and were asking me lots of questions. Now, a few weeks later, I find myself day dreaming about it. I have just got my signed shirt framed and hope to get all the other bits of memorabilia framed too."

Christmas Party.

To earn an invite to this most exclusive Christmas bash the JGs just had to enter a competition we ran in a matchday programme earlier this season. As usual all of the players turned up to join in the fun in the South Stand at Arsenal Stadium.

Everybody also had to turn up in fancy dress - this year the theme was fashions through the ages.

So as you can imagine we had our fair share of hippies and punks!! As well as meeting the players and getting a full film of photos and a full book of autographs, we also ran a few competitions on the day. We gave prizes for the best fancy dress and also held a raffle. Tom Sait was the compere for the afternoon and he entertained everybody with some magic tricks and illusions. The players spent more than an hour with us and looked like they enjoyed it as much as we did!

Our friends from Lens

You may have read before about the special friendship we have with RC Lens from France. Each season we invite our French friends over to Highbury for a game and the JGs really enjoy a 'reciprocal visit' to northern France. Last season we went to see Lens play Guingamp. The hospitality is always amazing in France and the JGs can't wait to say au revoir to London and head across the channel. At the Leeds game on May 4 it was the turn of the Lens Junior Supporters Club to come to Highbury. Just like the Arsenal fans the French were desperate for a Gunners win

but it wasn't to be. But it was still a great trip for the fans from Lens and at the end of the match it was made even more special when loads of the Arsenal players came pitch-side to sign autographs and let the Lens kids practise their English! Arsenal's on-loan 'keeper Guillaume Warmuz played for Lens for many years and he was absolutely thrilled to see some of his friends from home. He's even still the patron for the Lens Junior Supporters Club!

Ice is Easy

Gunnersaurus took a break from the green grass of Highbury to play football with some of his mascot mates on the white ice of the London Knights Ice Hockey team. Here is a report on his excellent day at the London Arena.

"I was invited, along with some of my other mascot friends, to the London Arena at Docklands by the Mighty Knight, the mascot of the London Knights Ice Hockey Team. I met up with the Wharf Canary, Bodger from Wycombe Wanderers, Buck and Dusty from the London Broncos, Billy Blood Drop, Theo from Leyton Orient and Gimmie from the English Netball Association. We all went out to greet the 5,000 plus crowd at the Main Entrance as they arrived to see the London Knights play the Belfast Giants.

"The highlight of the evening, was a game of ice football where yours truly played as goal-minder and despite letting in an early goal after 10 seconds (I wasn't ready, I was still taking up my position in goal when they scored!!). I performed heroics keeping the score down to 1-0. It was nice to see quite a few Gooners in the crowd cheering me on.

After the final whistle, we all had a rest and then went to sign autographs and have our pictures taken. This was the first time I had ever been on ice and do hope that I will be invited back, as I had such a great time."

As you can tell by the photos, Gunner had great fun, and probably didn't concede many goals because he fills the whole goal by lying down!!

They decided to use a white ball for the game though - see if you can spot it against the white ice!

All about Junior Gunners Membership.

Junior Gunners is a fan club for both boys and girls of sixteen years of age or less. (Sixteen years or less on August 31st 2003).

Membership fees are:
UK - £14 Overseas - £18 (Europe, Republic of Ireland and rest of the world).

Members receive: A membership card.
A colour photograph.
Newsletter sent to you 3 times a season.
Souvenir Pack.
A chance to purchase tickets at a reduced rate in the family.
enclosure subject to availability.
Discount on membership to the Travel Club.
A chance to be Arsenal's mascot - drawn at random.
Various competitions, quizzes and events held throughout the season.

If you are not already a Junior Gunner member, then why not give the Junior Gunners office a call on 0207 704 4160 and they will send you a membership form. Or you can look them up on the Arsenal website www.arsenal.com or e-mail them at juniorgunners@arsenal.co.uk.

Arsenal Club Football -
Your club, your life, your video game!

As you may know the Gunners have got their very own official video game! Arsenal Club Football is out for PlayStation 2 and Xbox and puts you on the pitch and into the action.

In Arsenal Club Football you can play alongside Bergkamp, Cole, Pires, Henry and all your heroes at Highbury. You can even put yourself in the game and play as part of the team with your name on the back of your shirt and hear it yelled by match commentators.

Imagine: its match day and you walk out onto the pitch at Highbury with the rest of the team; take on the opposition and score the winning goal. The stadium erupts with chants, drums and banners celebrating your win with the rest of the Arsenal team. In Arsenal Club Football your dreams of glory come true.

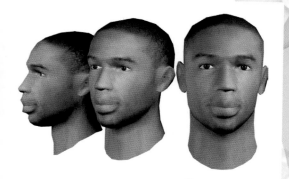

As it's the only official Arsenal video game, everything is perfectly captured in great detail – the first-team squad, the real kits, the real match day atmosphere and Arsene Wenger!

Arsenal stars get digitised!

Arsenal Club Football has the most recognisable and detailed Arsenal players in any football video game. Every player from the first team has had their face, head, hair and height individually modelled and digitised for the game and play in the proper world-famous Gunners strip.

These amazing player likenesses were captured by artists who visited the club and met all the players. Using 360-degree digital photography of each player's head, the images were processed into high-resolution graphics for the game, creating a perfect 3D model of the players.

It's just like being at Highbury

Arsenal Club Football also captures the

excitement and atmosphere of real matches when you play at Highbury. The stadium is accurately modelled from architectural drawings and detailed photographs, right down to the genuine hoardings and banners. The crowd chant club songs that you know from match days and there's TV-style commentary from footballing favourites Gary Lineker and Barry Davies throughout the matches.

Play in England and then onto Europe!
The game includes English Domestic Season, a European Super League and Custom game modes.

Play the Domestic Season as a League or a Knockout competition as you take on teams from the top two English divisions. As the season runs, the game lets you know how you're doing with a weekly summary of team and player stats.

The Super League delivers international club football played in two group stages (made up of 12 teams) followed by a knockout. Whether playing home or away, every match is in the official stadium of the host club, complete with highly detailed players.

The Custom Mode allows you to play fantasy football, creating Matches and Competitions with any of the hundreds of other clubs in the game. You can even create a whole team of fictional players (maybe with all your mates!) and design their looks and skills and choose your own team name.

Open the Arsenal Trophy Room!
Play well and you'll unlock special Arsenal features in the game's Trophy Room. In the Trophy Room, there's loads of Arsenal info detailing past honours, historic moments, along with first-team player stats, profiles and photos. If you play really well you can also see real-life video clips and photos of Arsenal's greatest moments.

With brilliant gameplay and all the Arsenal detail you need, Arsenal Club Football is the ultimate football action video game for every Gunners fan. It's now out on PlayStation 2 and Xbox and you can find out more about the game on the website at:
www.codemasters.com/arsenal

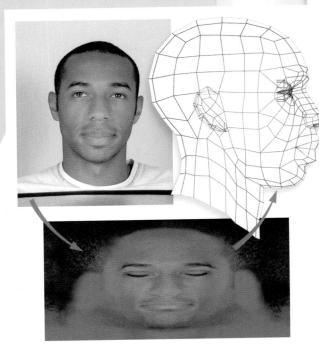

THE YOUNG GUNS' HQ

Whilst players from the Under 17s to the first team squad are based at Colney, the state-of-the-art Training Centre in Hertfordshire, players from nine years of age to sixteen are also able to develop within Shenley, the amazing facilities at Hale End which opened in 2001.

Ex-Arsenal Hero and now Head of Youth Development, Liam Brady tells of how important the training facility is. "Hale End has been a magnificent addition to the Academy set up," says Liam. "Prior to the facility opening we had to rent pitches to play our Academy fixtures. Some academies will have all the kids together from the Under 9s to the second year scholars, but we thought it was important to have a dedicated Academy for schoolboys away from the main Academy which caters for our scholars at the Training Centre. The schoolboys do get a feel of Shenley from time-to-time with games over there and as far as possible we have tried to make the facilities at Hale End like a 'mini-Shenley'."

"At 16 some youngsters will be taken on as scholars in the part of the Academy that's based at the Training Centre, but prior to that everything revolves around Hale End. It provides a top class base for our young players. The standard of pitches is right up there with the Shenley and Highbury surfaces and we now have a top notch artificial pitch there too."

The main aim of the set-up is to supply the next generation of Arsenal heroes. The most prominent example of a player progressing through the current system is Ashley Cole (pictured right at the Arsenal Soccer School), who has established himself as first choice left-back for both club and country. Stuart Taylor, Jermaine Pennant, Jeremie Aliadiere, David Bentley, Ryan Garry, Sebastian Svard and Moritz Volz have all appeared in the first team squad over the past year, progressing from the Arsenal Academy. There are also numerous former Arsenal Academy players who are using the excellent experience gained with the Gunners to carve out

promising professional careers at other clubs.

'We have a lot of good boys in the system and hopefully they'll play for the first team one day." adds Liam.

As Head of Youth Development, Brady is ultimately responsible for these youngsters but the man charged with the day-to-day management is former footballer and qualified teacher Roy Massey. Massey oversees more than 100 young footballers at Hale End. Here is his Academy low-down:

▶ To be part of the Hale End Academy you have to be local to Arsenal. Under 9s to Under 12s must live within an hour of Highbury. Under 12 to Under 16s must live within 90 minutes of Highbury.

▶ The FA's stipulation that youngsters can only play 30 games a season means that Arsenal Academy players rarely get the chance to play for their schools, as we play 24 games a season. We do, however, maintain very good links with schools to help

our youngsters with their development programmes.

▶ Members of the Hale End Academy train at the facility twice-a-week and play matches on Sundays.

▶ All matches against other Academies are officially deemed as Friendlies. The aim of Academy football at this age is very much to aid development, it is not results led.

▶ The teams of ten go on tour and play in International tournaments where they have been very successful. They experience different footballing cultures and styles which is very inspiring.

▶ Our Under 9s, 10s and 11s play nine-a-side matches on smaller, especially marked-out pitches.

From Under 12s the boys play 11-a-side matches.

▶ For nine-a-side games the youngsters usually play a 3-3-2 formation.

▶ Each coach takes a team for two years, allowing continuity and stability for our young players. After two years we feel it's an appropriate time to freshen ideas with a new coach with different expertise.

▶ Our first intake of eight year-olds for our Under 9 team is sourced from six development centres around London who have been working with youngsters from the age of seven.

▶ Those taken on as Under 9s are given two years to prove themselves at the Academy before a decision is made on their long term future. We aim to have drawn together the very best youngsters by the Under 12s, as by this age, the vast majority of players in London will be affiliated to either an Academy or School of Excellence at another club.

▶ We do still find youngsters at 12, 13 or 14 but these are boys who have played very little football until that age and their talent has shone through later than most.

Did you know?

The most prestigious competition for the nation's youngsters is the F.A. Youth Cup, played at Under 18 level. Arsenal has won the F.A. Youth Cup six times.

TRAINING GROUND SECRETS

Arsenal's state-of-the-art Training Centre is the envy of club and national teams around the world. The Centre is decked out with the latest gymnasium equipment, machines that aid in the rehabilitation of injured players, offices for the management staff, classrooms, press rooms and a restaurant that caters for the special dietary requirements of the players. Indoors the facility also contains three changing rooms, a steam room, a swimming pool with adjustable floor, treatment rooms and massage baths. Opened in 1999, the Shenley site boasts some of the best playing surfaces in the country.

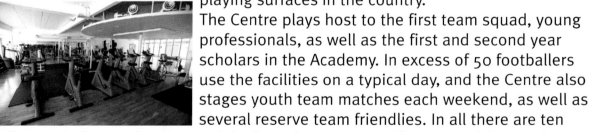

The Centre plays host to the first team squad, young professionals, as well as the first and second year scholars in the Academy. In excess of 50 footballers use the facilities on a typical day, and the Centre also stages youth team matches each weekend, as well as several reserve team friendlies. In all there are ten full-size pitches at the site, each built to the exact specifications of the playing surface at Highbury.

Of the ten pitches two have underground heating, and all are maintained by multiple award winning groundsman Steve Braddock and his team.

The existing Training Centre replaces the former University College London Union's site at London Colney, which was nurtured and developed from 1961 until 1999. Manager Arsène Wenger was a key figure in the development of the present Centre, in fact the contents and lay-out of the building were almost entirely decided by Arsène and his staff.

The physiotherapy team, led by Gary Lewin, had complete control over what the site would require for their crucial work, and fitness coach Tony Colbert, working in conjunction with Life Fitness (UK), equipped the gymnasium with everything necessary to keep the players in perfect condition.

The private Centre, provides an area of peace and relaxation for the players. As well as the playing and coaching staff, two full-time gardeners, 10 groundstaff, four catering staff, three building supervisors, and the manager's secretary are also based at Shenley. The Training Centre covers an area of 143 acres, including 45 acres of forestry.

We chatted with the Training Centre Manager, Sean O'Connor, and asked him a few questions about the training ground and how it is used throughout the year:

How many teams are catered for at the Training Centre?

We have four teams at the Centre. Under 17s, Under 19s, Reserves, first team - that's about 80 players in total; quite a few to look after as I'm sure you'll agree! In school holidays we also have 20 staff and the Under 16s who come to experience the way the seniors train.

What are your priorities in terms of managing both the facilities and the requirements of the players?

Our priority is to prepare for games and also to ensure a speedy recovery of the players. The managing of the facilities has to be first class. This includes looking after all the training pitches, the catering in the restaurant and ensuring that all the food that the players eat is healthy and of an excellent standard, the gym facilities are well maintained, the swimming pool is clean. This is Arsenal Football Club there is no other standard.

How do you and your staff keep the players happy?

We try to help players in any way we can. For example we can help them fill in the appropriate forms if they are from abroad. We have even helped players if they have problems with their cars!

What is the strangest request that an Arsenal player has ever put through to you?

The best so far was by David Seaman to put fish in our lake so that he could fish after training!

What kind of feedback have AFC players given you about the facilities at the Training Centre?

They all say they feel comfortable and at ease that's very important, and that the facilities are the best they have ever experienced.

Cleanliness at the Training Centre obviously holds great importance - how do you maintain such high levels of sanitation?

Arsène Wenger is very sharp on cleanliness, so my assistant Joe Da Silva has a team of six who clean the building top to bottom everyday. We also have a very strict policy when it comes to footwear. Any guests visiting the training ground have to wear plastic covers over their shoes so that no unwanted germs find their way into the changing rooms. Similarly all the staff at the training ground only wear indoor shoes to help maintain the level the Manager requires.

The Arsenal Training Centre has had some important visitors over the past few years, can you recall any interesting comments or reactions from these visitors?

Most of the reactions we get from players you see on their faces as they arrive, they are simply left in disbelief at the quality of the state of the art facilities. For example when Brazil came to England a couple of years ago, a number of squad members told Silvinho (the ex Arsenal full back) he was the luckiest player from Brazil, because he's here every day! They also said that the pitches were the best they had ever seen or played on in the world that's good enough for me.
There have been a host of international teams that have trained here including England senior and under 21s: Brazil, Germany, Ukraine, Scotland, Ivory Coast and Argentina.

How do you intend do keep the high standards at Arsenal's Training Centre?

Well I can't give you too much information because we wouldn't want to give our secrets away! However I will say that we set ourselves a five year plan when we came to the new centre and we are on schedule. We must continue to move forward if we are to remain the best in the country, if not Europe.

Can you tell us a little bit about the size of the site?

The site is 143 acres in size. 45 acres is new planted trees some 20,000, 30 acres of pitches, ten pitches in number, two lakes full of wild life and the rest is landscape and fields.

CAN YOU BELIEVE YOUR EYES?

1. DAVID PLATT WORE AN ARSENAL SHIRT YEARS BEFORE HE PLAYED FOR THEM

Pictured is former Arsenal midfielder David Platt sporting David Seaman's spare shirt at Highbury on April 3, 1991. Arsenal were 4-0 up over Aston Villa and on their way to a 5-0 win when Villa 'keeper Nigel Spink injured his arm in a challenge with Kevin Campbell. The injury ended Spink's match and also prevented him from removing his shirt to give to stand in 'keeper Platt who had to borrow one of Seaman's, his England team-mate. Bruce Rioch brought him back to Highbury to play in a Gunners shirt, this time as an Arsenal player.

2. NORTH LONDON EASTENDERS:

It's the summer of 1987 and the country is gripped by new soap opera Eastenders. One of the soap stars at the time was fruit and veg salesman Pete Beale. An archetypal Cockney, with the catchphrase 'alright, treacle?' Beale was occasionally seen with a West Ham scarf tucked under his sheepskin coat. The majority of characters in Eastenders seem to support either the Hammers or of course Walford Town, but in real life many of the cast, past and present, are staunch Gunners fans, including Peter Dean (Pete) himself, Susan Tully (Michelle), Tom Watt (Lofty), Tamsin Outhwaite (Mel), Lucy Speed (Natalie), Patsy Palmer (Bianca) and Sid Owen (Ricky). For this picture Dean reversed roles with Arsenal stars Kenny Sansom and Graham Rix. The fruit and veg salesman dons the Gunners kit whilst Sansom and Rix go for the 'barrow boy look'.

3. IT'S NOT EVERY DAY YOU FINISH A MATCH IN THE KNOWLEDGE THAT YOU'VE JUST SECURED THE FIRST LEAGUE AND CUP 'DOUBLE' IN 27 YEARS FOR ARSENAL.

David Seaman literally jumped for joy in the Wembley changing rooms after the celebrations had finished on the pitch. You can see Gilles Grimandi, Nicolas Anelka and Tony Adams laughing at the keeper's antics.

HIGHBURY HOBBIES

WHO IS YOUR FAVOURITE SPORTSMAN OR WOMAN OUTSIDE OF FOOTBALL?

ASHLEY COLE -
Shaquille O'Neil (Basketball)
FREDDIE LJUNGBERG -
Michael Jordan (Basketball)
DENNIS BERGKAMP -
Michael Jordan (Basketball)
THIERRY HENRY -
Michael Jordan (Basketball)

WHAT WOULD YOU BE IF YOU WEREN'T A FOOTBALLER?

DENNIS BERGKAMP –
Physiotherapist
FREDDIE LJUNGBERG –
Fighter Pilot
ASHLEY COLE –
Anything else in sport
THIERRY HENRY –
I'd probably play basketball

BOYHOOD HERO:

FREDDIE LJUNGBERG -
Socrates (Brazil)
DENNIS BERGKAMP -
Johan Cruyff (Netherlands)
ASHLEY COLE -
David Rocastle (ex-Arsenal)
THIERRY HENRY -
Marco Van Basten (Netherlands)

FAVOURITE HOLIDAY DESTINATION:

FREDDIE LJUNGBERG -
Great Barrier Reef in Australia
DENNIS BERGKAMP -
France
ASHLEY COLE -
Las Vegas
THIERRY HENRY -
West Indies, it holds a special place in my heart.

FAVOURITE TV SHOW:

FREDDIE LJUNGBERG -
Only Fools and Horses
DENNIS BERGKAMP –
Friends
ASHLEY COLE -
Eastenders

BOYHOOD TEAM:

FREDDIE LJUNGBERG -
Swedish team, Halmstads
DENNIS BERGKAMP -
Ajax
ASHLEY COLE -
Arsenal

BEST CITY:

FREDDIE LJUNGBERG -
London
DENNIS BERGKAMP -
Amsterdam
ASHLEY COLE -
London

CLASSIC DERBY VICTORIES

Last season, Arsenal gave their most accomplished display in a north London derby for many years with a 3-0 victory over Spurs at Highbury. Here we look at other great moments and some not so great for Arsenal in north London derbies:

▶ In the 1934/35 season Arsenal were on their way to a third consecutive title and Spurs were in the process of being relegated. In October 1934, Ted Drake grabbed a hat-trick at Highbury as Arsenal won 5-1. At White Hart Lane just over four months later, Drake grabbed two more in a 6-0 win. That's still the biggest win in a north London derby.

▶ On the morning of 16 September 1967, the best man at George Graham's wedding was Spurs midfielder Terry Venables. That afternoon, Graham slid Arsenal's third goal as they beat Spurs 4-0 in a league match at Highbury.

▶ On 3 May 1971, Ray Kennedy's last-gasp header at White Hart Lane won the match 1-0 and also clinched the League Championship. Five days later, the Gunners beat Liverpool 2-1 in The FA Cup Final at Wembley to complete the 'double'.

▶ In December 1978, Liam Brady inspired a memorable 5-0 away win over Spurs, with striker Alan Sunderland scoring a hat-trick.

In April 1983 Spurs got their revenge and reversed the scoreline to win 5-0 at White Hart Lane.

In 1987, three outstanding League Cup Semi-Finals took place between Arsenal and Tottenham Hotspur. Spurs won 1-0 in the first leg at Highbury. In the second leg at White Hart Lane Tottenham striker Clive Allen netted again to give Spurs a 2-0 aggregate lead. Arsenal were inspired in the second-half, with Viv Anderson and Niall Quinn scoring to force extra time and a replay. A toss was then made for the venue for the third match, Spurs won it and the match was therefore played at White Hart Lane. Clive Allen struck again but with eight minutes left Ian Allison tucked away a close-range effort to ensure a furious finale. With time running out, a shot from Allison rebounded into the path of David Rocastle, who ran on to stroke Arsenal's winner past Ray Clemence to earn a famous victory. In the League Cup Final, the Gunners came back from behind again to beat Liverpool 2-1 at Wembley, courtesy of two goals from Charlie Nicholas.

In 1991, Arsenal and Spurs met in the FA Cup Semi-Final at Wembley. It was Spurs midfielder Paul Gascoigne's match. Tottenham manager Terry Venables gambled on semi-fit Gazza and was rewarded when he scored a magnificent free-kick goal past David Seaman. Gary Lineker stabbed home Spurs' second. Alan Smith headed in Lee Dixon's cross to revive Arsenal hopes, but Lineker's breakaway goal won the contest.

Two years later, in 1993 the north London rivals met at Wembley again in another FA Cup Semi-Final. This time, a goal from Tony Adams decided the match in a 1-0 victory for the Gunners. With ten minutes left, the Arsenal captain stole in unmarked at the far post to bury Paul Merson's free-kick with a stooping header.

In the spring of 2001, the two teams again crossed paths in an FA Cup Semi-Final, this time at Old Trafford. In this match, Spurs took an early lead but Arsenal attacked relentlessly for the remainder of the game and won 2-1 with goals from Patrick Vieira and Robert Pires.

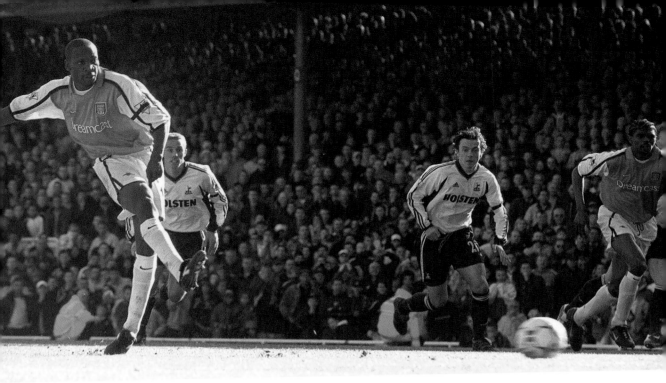

▶ On 6 April 2002, Arsenal had reason to celebrate when they beat their neighbours 2-1 at Highbury to go back to the top of the Premiership table and a step closer to what would become Arsenal's third 'double'. This match was won by a late penalty from Lauren, who coolly rolled the ball into the net from the spot.

▶ In Arsenal's 3-0 league win at Highbury in the 131st north London derby in November 2002, Vieira controlled midfield, Dennis Bergkamp bewitched the Spurs defence and Sol Campbell was solid at the back. But it was the performance of Thierry Henry, and a goal after 13 minutes which stole the show. The Frenchman picked up the ball on the edge of his own penalty area and carried it over 70 yards, tricking his way past a succession of Spurs defenders before sending a measured shot beyond Tottenham goalkeeper Kasey Keller. The goal was voted as the 'ITV Goal of the Season' for 2002/2003.

No doubt the next 100 years will provide more exciting moments from north London derbies.

Arsenal
OVERSEAS PLAYERS

Iceland

Faroe Islands

Sw

Denma

Netherlands

France

United States of America

Ivory Coast   Nige

Brazil

In recent seasons Arsenal has seen a real influx of talent from all over the globe. The Club has players that come from as far away as the Ivory Coast in West Africa, to Latvia which is in Eastern Europe, to Brazil in South America.
To help show the mix of nationalities that are represented in the Arsenal squad we have drawn up a map of the world which shows exactly where Arsenal's multi-national and multi-talented squad comes from, proving that Arsenal really are a global team.

FRANCE
Patrick Vieira
Robert Pires
Sylvain Wiltord
Thierry Henry
Pascal Cygan
Jeremie Aliadiere
Gael Clichy

SCANDINAVIA
Fredrik Ljungberg (Sweden
Sebastian Larsson (Sweden)
Ingi Hojsted (Faroe Islands)
Olafur-Ingi Skulason (Iceland)
Sebastian Svard (Denmark)
Rami Shaaban (Sweden)

LATVIA
Igors Stepanovs

NETHERLANDS
Giovanni van Bronckhorst
Dennis Bergkamp

GREECE
Stathis Tavlaridis

GERMANY
Moritz Volz
Jens Lehmann

SWITZERLAND
Philippe Senderos

AFRICA
Lauren (Cameroon)
Kanu (Nigeria)
Kolo Toure (Ivory Coast)

BRAZIL
Gilberto
Edu
Juan

UNITED STATES OF AMERICA
Frankie Simek

France

Patrick Vieira – Patrick has been ever present in the French national squad since 1998 and is as important to France as he is to Arsenal. When Patrick played against Russia in April 2002 he set a new record for consecutive international appearances for his country. He was a key member of the squad that won the 1998 World Cup in France as well as the Euro 2000 triumph a couple of years later.

Thierry Henry – As mirrored in his early club career Thierry played a number of games for France as a wide player as opposed to his now familiar striking role. In the 1998 World Cup triumph he was used as a winger throughout much of the tournament, but during the Euro 2000 success Thierry moved to a central striking role with instant success. He was voted man of the tournament in the 2003 Confederations Cup after some great performances and a number of goals to his name as well.

Sylvain Wiltord –Sylvain has a knack of scoring important and memorable goals for both club and country, arguably his most important goal for his country was in Semi-Final of the Euro 2000 competition against Italy. Sylvain is a key member of the current French squad and his versatility means that he is comfortable playing in midfield or as a centre forward.

Robert Pires – Arsenal's magical number 7, Robert Pires returned to International football at the end of 2002 with the friendly fixture against the Czech Republic. After his long injury lay off, he is now back as a regular feature in the French squad and he was bestowed the honour of captaining his country for the first time in the recent Confederations Cup game against Japan. He led by example, scoring the opening goal in a 2-1 win.

Pascal Cygan – Pascal was a summer signing at the beginning of the 2002/2003 season from Lille where he skippered the side. Pascal has yet to win a cap for France but was voted the most consistent player in the French league the season before he joined Arsenal.

Jeremie Aliadiere – Jeremie is a graduate of the famous Clairefontaine Academy in France and is regarded as one of the hottest prospects at Highbury, he is also a French Under-21 International. The youngster made a great start to last season, scoring at Highbury against West Bromwich Albion, but the remainder of the campaign was blighted by injury but he'll be happy to establish himself in 2003/2004.

Gael Clichy - French full-back Gael Clichy joined Arsenal from French National League side AS Cannes. The 18 year-old impressed when on trial with the club pre-season 2003/2004, having joined the first team at their Austrian training camp at the end of July. Clichy featured in all of the Club's seven pre-season friendlies, and over the coming seasons will hopefully be another Frenchman to make his mark at Highbury.

Sweden

Fredrik Ljungberg – Freddie is a key member of the Swedish national side being deployed as an attacking midfielder who is encouraged to get forward as much as possible. He represented Sweden at the 2002 World Cup in Japan and Korea and he helped them top their group. Freddie has been ever present in Sweden's Euro 2004 qualifying campaign.

Sebastian Larsson – Sebastian is a central midfielder with a growing reputation both at Arsenal and at Swedish youth level. At just 18 years of age he looks as if he has a bright future ahead of him and he will be looking to try and emulate the success of his fellow countryman, Freddie Ljungberg, in both Arsenal and Swedish colours.

Rami Shaaban –Rami was bought to Arsenal from Swedish side Durgarden at the beginning of the 2002/2003 season after a successful 'double' winning season with his hometown club. Rami enjoys dual nationality having a Finnish mother and an Egyptian father which could allow him to pursue other international options later in his career.

Faroe Islands

Ingi Hojsted - Arsenal's youthful Faroese central midfielder has had an injury plagued start to his career at the Club. However he enjoyed his debut for Faroe Islands in 2003 when they beat Kazakhstan 2-1, the 17 year old came on as a second-half substitute. Ingi also featured in the Euro 2004 qualifying game against Germany in which the Faroe Islands looked poised to celebrate a famous victory until two late goals by the 2002 World Cup Finalists.

Iceland

Olafur-Ingi Skulason – This young Icelandic midfielder has been at Arsenal since 2001 when he was signed from his previous club Fylkir AC. He started out as a right-back but has progressed into a strong midfield player and although he has played for Iceland's under 20's national side he has yet to receive a call up for the full national squad.

Latvia

Igors Stepanovs – Igors is a regular in the Latvian national side playing in his favoured centre-back position. Known as 'The Latvian Beckenbauer' in his homeland, Igors has been instrumental in Latvia's great strides towards qualification for the the 2004 European Championship Finals in Portugal.

Denmark

Sebastian Svard – The powerful Danish youngster is widely tipped to make a great impact at both Arsenal and for his native Denmark. Comfortable across the back-line as well as in central midfield, Seb has represented his country at junior levels and recently graduated to the Under-21 set-up.

Germany

Moritz Volz – The young German has represented his country at various age groups and has even captained the Under 19 national team on a number of occasions. The talented 20 year-old can operate either in midfield or at right full-back and loves to drive forward in support of the strikers from either position.

Jens Lehmann - Jens signed from German side Borussia Dortmund in the summer, and made his goalkeeping debut in the pre-season tour to Austria. He helped them to the 2002 Bundesliga title and played against Arsenal in last season's Champions League. Jens' other honours include the Uefa Cup which he lifted with Schalke in 1997. He made his Germany debut against Oman in 1998, and has now won 16 caps. He was a non-playing member of Germany's 1998 and 2002 World Cup squads.

Greece

Stathis Tavlaridis – Stathis was brought to Arsenal after an impressive performance for the U21 Greek national side against England U21's back in 2001. Stathis played a big part in helping Greece qualify for the U21 European Championships in 2002. Tall and strong, he can play as either a centre-back or as a full-back.

Brazil

Edu – Signed from the Brazilian team Corinthians back in January 2001 and although he suffered with a number of injuries earlier in his Arsenal career he has now blossomed into a tremendous asset to the squad. He has superb ball control, which coupled with his sweet left foot keeps the Highbury crowd enthralled whenever he plays. Yet to win a cap for his native Brazil it is surely only a matter of time before this talented midfielder converts his skills onto the International scene.

Gilberto – Like a number of his French colleagues in the Arsenal squad Gilberto knows what it is like to win a World Cup having been a vital member of Brazil's triumph in the 2002 competition, so vital in fact that he played every single minute of the tournament for the world champions. Gilberto's first season as a Gunner ended in success with an FA Cup Winners medal and he has forged a solid partnership with the skipper, Patrick Vieira, in the centre of Arsenal's midfield.

Juan - The diminutive Brazilian right-back joined Arsenal back in 2001 from his home town club, Sao Paulo. He made an impressive Gunners debut in an FA Cup victory against Gillingham and his attacking verve was a feature of the reserve team in his first season. His second season at the Club was hampered by a serious knee injury, though he'll be hopeful of re-establishing himself on the fringes of the first-team next season.

United States of America

Frankie Simek – The strong and solidly built American has been affiliated to Arsenal since he was 12 years old. He signed professionally with the Club back in the summer of 2002 and has been a key player for the youth teams at the Club. Frankie has also shown great promise whilst playing for the United States Under 20 team and he was a key member during their recent qualification for the U20 World Cup Finals.

Holland

Dennis Bergkamp – The mercurial Dutchman has been at Highbury for 8 seasons and in this time has thrilled the Arsenal fans with magnificent skill and flair. Dennis also had a fantastic International career for Holland and when retired from International football in 1998 after the World Cup Finals in France he had won 79 caps for his country and had scored 39 goals, a goal scoring record that was only recently broken by the Barcelona front man, Patrick Kluivert.

Giovanni van Bronckhorst – An experienced International with a cultured left foot, Gio has proved to be an invaluable member of the Arsenal squad. In his two years at the Club he has already acquired a Championship medal and two FA Cup winners' medals. Yet to taste success on the International stage, Gio is a regular for the super-talented Netherlands team who already look odds on for Euro 2004 qualification.

Switzerland

Philippe Senderos - Philippe joined Arsenal during the summer. The highly rated central defender was chased by a number of high profile clubs before the 18 year-old decided to leave Servette for Highbury. Philippe was the captain of the Switzerland side that won the 2001/2002 UEFA European Under-17 Championship. He has also won caps at Under-21 level for his country. He made his Gunners debut in the pre-season friendly match at Peterborough.

Cameroon

Lauren – The Gunners right-back has had a number of highlights in his International career, including helping Cameroon to victory in the 2002 African Nations Cup, repeating the success he enjoyed with his country in the same competition in 2000. He also can add the gold medal he won in the 2000 Sydney Olympic Games to his total haul of International honours. He was also a key member of the Cameroon side that played in the 2002 World Cup Finals where he played in a central midfield role. Lauren made the decision to retire from international football last year.

Nigeria

Kanu – Arsenal's master of skill and trickery has proven to be a crucial member of Nigeria's 'Super Eagles' squad over recent years. The most notable success of his International career came when he helped Nigeria to a gold medal at the 1996 Atlanta Olympic Games when they defeated pre-tournament favourites, Argentina, in the Final. Kanu was given the captain's armband in 2001 and has enjoyed that role since, leading his country in both the African Nations Cup and the World Cup in 2002.

Ivory Coast

Kolo Toure – The powerful Ivorian made his International debut back in April 2000 against Rwanda and since then has been an integral part of the national side. Kolo joined Arsenal from one of the top club teams in African football, Asec Mimosas at the beginning of 2002. Kolo has played in a number of different positions since joining Arsenal but is regularly used as a central defender for the Ivory Coast.

FORMER OVERSEAS PLAYERS

Its not just in recent years that Arsenal have been well represented by foreign players, here we highlight a number of overseas footballers that have pulled on the famous red and white Arsenal shirt.

JUNICHI INAMOTO
JAPAN, 2001-2002

NELSON VIVAS
ARGENTINA, 1998-2001

ALEX MANNINGER
AUSTRIA, 1997-2001

VLADIMIR PETROVIC
YUGOSLAVIA, 1982 - 1983

CHRISTOPHER WREH
LIBERIA, 1997 - 2000

JOHN KOSMINA
AUSTRALIA, 1978 -1979

LUIS BOA MORTE
PORTUGAL, 1997-1999

JEHAD MUNTASSER
LIBYA, 1997-1998

PAL LYDERSEN
NORWAY, 1991-1995

BRENDAN BATSON
TRINIDAD & TOBAGO– 1968-1974

DANIEL LE RUOX
SOUTH AFRICA – 1957-1958